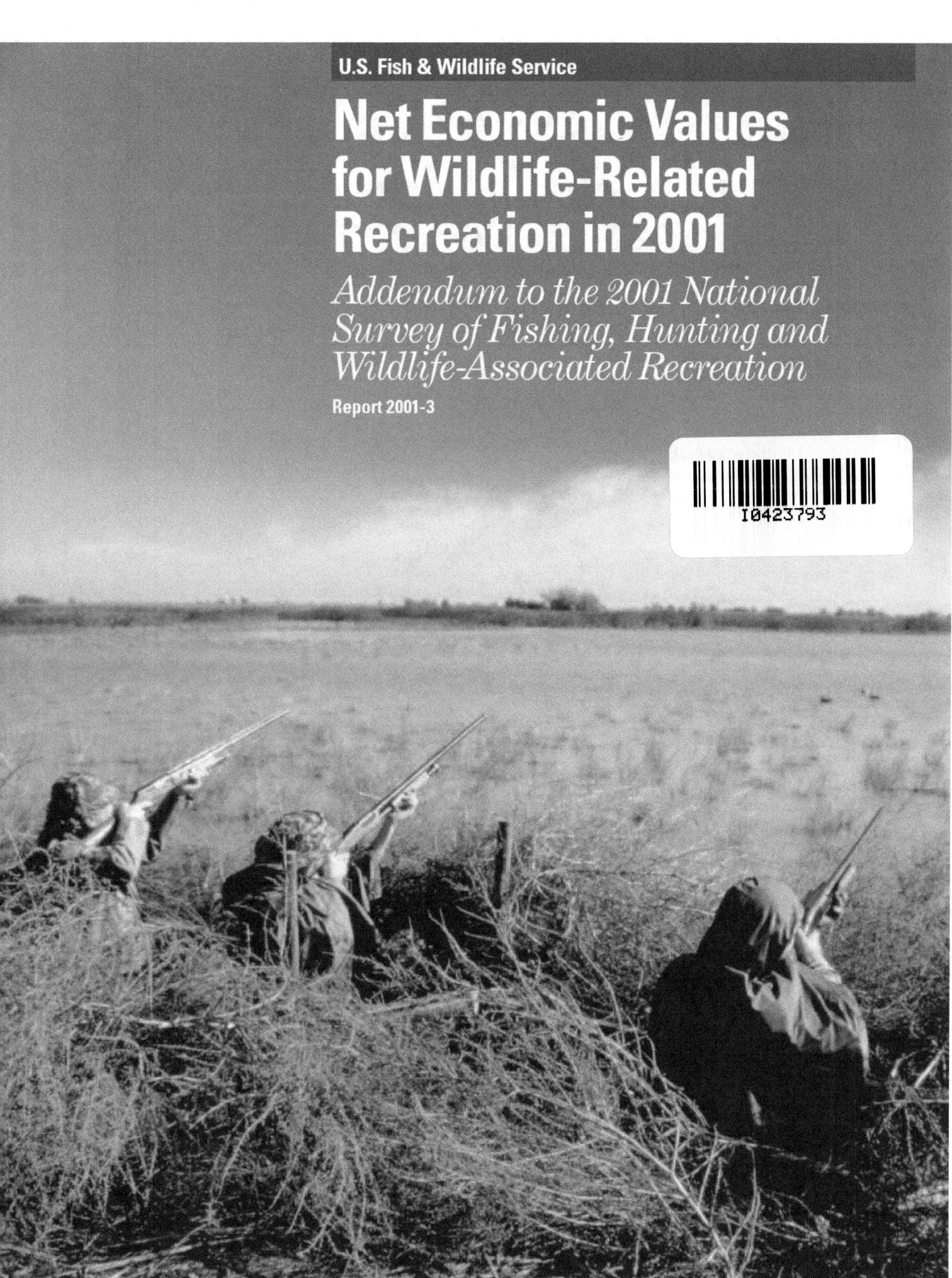

U.S. Fish & Wildlife Service

Net Economic Values for Wildlife-Related Recreation in 2001

Addendum to the 2001 National Survey of Fishing, Hunting and Wildlife-Associated Recreation

Report 2001-3

I0423793

U.S. Fish & Wildlife Service

Net Economic Values for Wildlife-Related Recreation in 2001

Addendum to the 2001 National Survey of Fishing, Hunting and Wildlife-Associated Recreation

Report 2001-3
September 2003

Richard Aiken and Genevieve Pullis La Rouche
Division of Federal Aid
U.S. Fish and Wildlife Service
Washington, D.C.

Division of Federal Aid
U.S. Fish and Wildlife Service
Washington, D.C. 20240
Director, Steve Williams
Chief, Division of Federal Aid, Kris La Montagne
http://fa.r9.fws.gov/

This report is intended to complement the National and State reports from the 2001 National Survey of Fishing, Hunting, and Wildlife-Associated Recreation. The conclusions are the authors and do not represent official positions of the U.S. Fish and Wildlife Service.

Contents

Abstract

This report presents state estimates of the net economic values for smallmouth and largemouth bass, trout and walleye fishing, deer, elk and moose hunting, and nonresidential wildlife watching. These values are based on contingent valuation questions from the 2001 National Survey of Fishing, Hunting, and Wildlife-Associated Recreation.

Each state was classified as either a bass, trout or walleye state. Based on these classifications, anglers were asked to answer a contingent valuation question for their bass, trout, or walleye fishing during 2001.

Likewise, each state was classified as either a deer, elk or moose state. Based on these classifications, hunters were asked contingent valuation questions for their 2001 hunts.

People who took trips in 2001 to watch wildlife at least one mile from their residence were asked contingent valuation questions for these activities.

The net economic values reported here are developed for current resource conditions. They are appropriate measures of economic value for use in cost-benefit analyses, damage assessments, and project evaluations.

David Heffernan, USFWS

I. Introduction

The National Survey of Fishing, Hunting, and Wildlife-Associated Recreation (Survey hereafter) is a comprehensive source of data on people's use of wildlife resources that has been collected on a national level since 1955 and on a state level since 1975. The first time the Survey collected net economic value data was in 1980. The effort was repeated, with some changes, in the 1985, 1991, 1996, and 2001 Surveys.

This report presents estimates of net economic values for smallmouth and largemouth bass, trout and walleye fishing, deer, elk and moose hunting, and nonresidential wildlife watching. These values were derived from contingent valuation questions asked in the 2001 Survey. The report also compares the 2001 values with those of the 1980 and 1985 Surveys which used a similar contingent valuation methodology. Bass fishing refers to smallmouth and largemouth bass and excludes white bass, spotted bass, striped bass, striped bass hybrids, and rock bass. Trout fishing refers to all freshwater species commonly known as trout. Nonresidential wildlife watching refers to trips at least one mile from home taken for the primary purpose of observing, photographing, or feeding wildlife (wildlife watching hereafter).

The last five Surveys varied in the types of fishing and hunting asked for each state and in the methods and procedures used for contingent valuation. Regarding fishing, the 1980 Survey asked only trout fishing valuation questions for each state whereas the 1985 Survey asked only bass fishing valuation questions. The 1991 Survey assigned states as either primarily bass fishing or primarily trout fishing. A person who lived in a bass state was asked a bass fishing valuation question and was not asked a trout valuation question, and vice versa for a person who lived in a trout state. The 1996 and 2001 Surveys selected states in the upper Midwest as walleye states and the rest of the states as either trout fishing or bass fishing states.

In 1980, all states were designated both deer and waterfowl states for valuation questions. In 1985, all states again were designated both deer and waterfowl states, and elk hunting valuation questions were asked for the northwestern and northern Rocky Mountain states. In 1991, all states were designated as deer hunting. In 1996 and 2001 selected states in the northwest and northern Rocky Mountains were designated as elk states, Alaska was designated as a moose state, and the remainder as deer states.

Wildlife watching valuation questions were asked in 1985, 1991, 1996, and 2001. Respondents were asked about the trips they took for the primary purpose of observing, photographing, or feeding wildlife.

Another change in the Surveys deals with respondents' state-assigned activity status. When a person answered a valuation question in the 1991 and earlier Surveys, their valuation response was assigned to their state of residence. Thus, a person from Michigan who hunted deer would have their deer valuation response assigned to Michigan even if they hunted deer in another state (e.g., mule deer in Utah). In the 1996 and 2001 Surveys, responses were assigned to the state where the activity occurred. Thus, with the example above, the response by a person from Michigan who hunted deer in Utah would be assigned to Utah.

A third difference among the Surveys is the contingent valuation method itself. In 1980 and 1985, an open-ended approach was used, which essentially consisted of directly asking respondents how much was their total willingness to pay for a typical trip. In 1991 and 1996 a dichotomous choice method was used, in which the respondents were asked if they would have taken any trips if their total costs were some predetermined amount more than what they had actually paid. For the 2001 Survey, the open-ended approach was used again. Therefore

comparison of 2001 values with 1980 and 1985 values is a more reliable comparison than with 1991 and 1996 values because the valuation questions were similar.

The following section discusses the conceptual framework for net economic values of wildlife-related recreation, differentiating between net economic values and economic impacts. The third section describes the contingent valuation questions used in the Survey and steps that were taken in analyzing the data. The fourth section consists of value estimates for deer, elk and moose hunting, bass, trout and walleye fishing, and wildlife watching. This section also briefly compares the 2001 estimates with those from 1985 and 1980. The fifth section discusses how to use the value estimates presented, and the last section provides concluding comments.

II. Measures of Economic Value

In 2001 82 million Americans 16 years old and older fished, hunted, photographed, fed, and closely observed wildlife in the U.S. These wildlife enthusiasts spent $28.1 billion on trips to participate in these activities. Expenditures are a useful indicator of the importance of wildlife-related recreation to local, regional, and national economies. However, they do not measure the economic benefit to either the individual participant or, when aggregated, to society.

Expenditures and net economic values are two widely used but distinctly different measures of the economic value of wildlife-related recreation. Net willingness to pay, or "consumer surplus", is the accepted measure of the economic value of wildlife-related recreation to the individual recreationist and to society. It is the appropriate measure of economic value for a wide range of analyses that seek to quantify benefits and costs.

Net economic value is measured as participants' willingness to pay for wildlife-related recreation over and above what they actually spend to participate. The benefit to society is the summation of willingness to pay across all individuals. There is a direct relationship between expenditures and net economic value, as shown in Figure 1. A demand curve for a representative hunter is shown in the figure. An individual hunter's demand curve gives the number of trips the hunter would take per year for each different cost per trip. The downward sloping demand curve represents marginal willingness to pay per trip and indicates that each additional trip is valued less by the hunter than the preceding trip. All other factors being equal, the lower the cost per trip (vertical axis) the more trips the hunter will take (horizontal axis). The cost of a hunting trip serves as an implicit price for hunting since a market price generally does not exist for this activity. At $60 per trip, the hunter would choose not to hunt, but if hunting trips were free, the hunter would take 16 hunting trips.

At a cost per trip of $20 the hunter takes 10 trips, with a total willingness to pay of $375 (area acde in Figure 1). Total willingness to pay is the total value the hunter places on participation. The hunter will not take more than 10 trips because the cost per trip ($20) exceeds what he would pay for an additional trip. For each trip between zero and 10, however, the hunter would actually have been willing to pay more than $20 (the demand curve, showing marginal willingness to pay, lies above $20).

The difference between what the hunter is willing to pay and what is actually paid is net economic value. In this simple example, therefore, net economic value is $175 (($55 – $20) × 10 ÷ 2) (triangle bcd in Figure 1) and hunter expenditures are $200 ($20 × 10) (rectangle abde in Figure 1). Thus, the hunter's total willingness to pay is composed of net economic value and total expenditures. Net economic value is simply total willingness to pay minus expenditures. The relationship between net economic value and expenditures is the basis for asserting that net economic value is an appropriate measure of the benefit an individual derives from participation in an activity and that expenditures are not the appropriate benefit measure.

Expenditures are out-of-pocket expenses on items a hunter purchases in order to hunt. The remaining value, net willingness to pay (net economic value), is the economic measure of an individual's satisfaction after all costs of participation have been paid.

Summing the net economic values of all individuals who participate in an activity derives the value to society. For our example let us assume that there are 100 hunters who hunt at a particular wildlife management area and all have demand curves identical to that of our typical hunter presented in Figure 1. The total value per year of this wildlife management area to society is $17,500 ($175 × 100).

The example developed for hunting could have been developed in the context of fishing or wildlife watching. The basic concept of net economic value is the same for all three activities.

Figure 1. Individual Hunter's Demand Curve for Hunting Trips

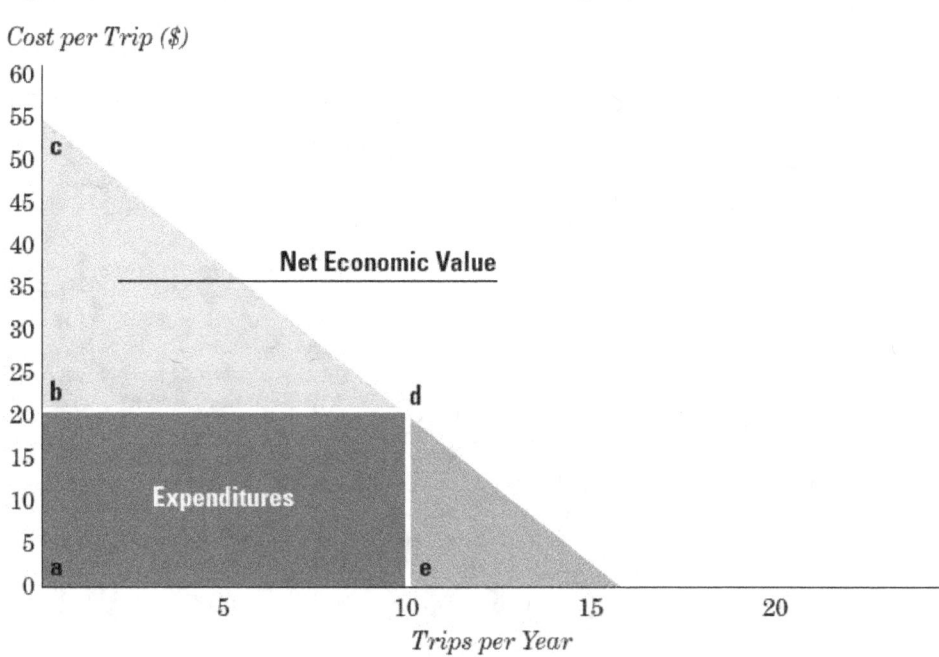

III. Contingent Valuation

Respondents to the 2001 Survey who had gone deer, elk or moose hunting, bass, trout, or walleye fishing, or wildlife watching were asked a series of contingent valuation (CV) questions during their personal interview as a basis for determining their net willingness to pay for those activities. Questions were designed to find the respondent's cost per trip in 2001, whether they would have continued to go had the cost been higher, and at what cost per trip they would not have gone at all in 2001 because it would have been too expensive (Appendix A presents the hunting and wildlife watching CV question series, as examples).

Respondents first were asked to estimate the number of trips they had taken in 2001 to hunt or fish for the designated species. For wildlife watching the number of trips was obtained from an earlier section of the questionnaire. Respondents then were asked to consider expenses such as transportation, food and lodging, and to estimate what their cost had been in 2001 for a typical trip[1]. Then they were asked at what cost per trip they would not have gone at all because it was too expensive. The question stipulated that the cost of other kinds of recreational activities that could be considered substitutes would not have changed.

In terms of Figure 1 the purpose of the question sequence is to have the respondent react as if he were moving up the demand curve, taking fewer trips as the cost per trip increased until he was priced out of the market at the cost per trip where the demand curve intersects the vertical axis. Assuming a linear demand curve, annual net economic value is then calculated using the difference between current cost ($20) and the maximum cost at the intercept ($55), and the number of trips taken in 2001 (10).

Using the example in Figure 1, annual net economic value is

$$\frac{(\$55 - \$20) \times 10}{2}$$
$$= \$175$$

The average value per trip is that amount divided by the number of trips, or

$$\$175 \div 10 = \$17.50 \text{ per trip}$$

The valuation sequence was posed in terms of number of trips and cost per trip because respondents were thought more likely to think of their wildlife-related recreation in terms of trips rather than days, the unit most commonly used in project evaluation. The economic values reported here are in terms of days to facilitate their use in analysis.

The values are averages in two senses of the word. First, they are the arithmetic mean of the responses of all respondents in the sample, usually all those residing in a particular state who participated in the activity, e.g., all survey respondents who were Colorado residents and hunted elk in Colorado. Second, they are average values in that they are calculated for each respondent by dividing his total annual consumer surplus for an activity by the number of days he participated during 2001.

Zero and negative net willingness-to-pay responses were deleted from the analysis, as were unreasonably high willingness-to-pay responses. Likely explanations of zero and negative willingness to pay are that the question was misunderstood by the respondent, incorrectly recorded by the interviewer, or that the response was a protest against higher costs rather than a legitimate bid, perhaps motivated by fear of an increase in the cost of a hunting or fishing license. To the extent that legitimate zero responses were among those deleted, the resulting values will be overestimates.

Jim Palmer, USFWS

Willingness to pay for wildlife-related recreation or, for that matter, anything a consumer buys, must be limited by some measure of an individual's income and/or wealth. A person clearly is not able to pay some multiple of his household's annual income for deer hunting, for example. In a less extreme situation, it is possible that a truly avid deer hunter would actually be willing to pay a significant portion of his income to continue hunting deer even though the costs of substitute activities such as small game hunting would be unchanged. Since the purpose of the analysis is to use the CV responses as representative of the typical recreationist in the group rather than calculating the sample's aggregate net economic value, mitigating the effect of those extreme values on the sample mean is essential. Observations were dropped from the samples if the annual net economic value for an activity exceeded five percent of the individual's household income.

---

[1] Wildlife watchers were given the dollar figure per trip which they had reported earlier in the interview. If the respondent did not think this was accurate he or she could change it.

IV. Estimated Net Economic Values

Tables 1 through 7 give state-by-state net economic values and standard errors for a day of deer, elk and moose hunting, bass, trout, and walleye fishing, and wildlife watching. There are several important things to know about the estimates. They are mean responses for net economic value per day based on the respondent's state of activity. Each table gives the values of state residents and nonresidents.

Because they are based on samples of recreationists, the values in the tables are estimates of the true population means and should be considered in relation to their standard errors and corresponding confidence intervals. The 95 percent confidence intervals are the estimated mean plus or minus roughly two times the standard error of the mean. Confidence intervals serve as indicators of the reliability of estimates. A 95 percent confidence interval means that the true value falls within that range in 95 out of 100 samples of the same size. An example of the use of the 95 percent confidence interval is the seemingly large difference in the mean value of a day of deer hunting by Texas residents ($76 per day) in comparison with that of Oklahoma residents ($56 per day). In reality the two values are not statistically different because their 95 percent confidence intervals overlap.

Sample sizes and the degree of variation of responses within the samples are the primary reasons that some state confidence intervals are narrower than others. Sample sizes varied significantly across states. Values are not reported based on samples of less than ten observations.

Eugene Hester, USFWS

In all the tables, there is substantial variation in mean value from one state to the next even after deleting extreme responses. Confidence intervals can help in interpreting these apparent differences. For example, the 95 percent confidence interval of the Kansas state resident bass fishing per day mean ($13 to $29) and that of the mean in neighboring Oklahoma ($18 to $48) overlap. Thus, the two means ($20 for Kansas and $33 for Oklahoma) are not statistically different at that level of significance. However, the 95% confidence intervals for Kansas ($13 to $29) and Missouri ($30 to $76) do not overlap, so the difference in the means for Kansas ($20) and Missouri ($52) bass fishing net economic values can be interpreted as a true difference.

Table 1. Deer Hunting Net Economic Values Per Day: 2001

	State Resident Values			Out-of-Stater's Values		
	Dollars per Day	Standard Error	95% Confidence Interval	Dollars per Day	Standard Error	95% Confidence Interval
Aggregate	56	2	52-60	76	8	61-92
Alabama	110*	30	51-169	57*	41	−24-138
Arizona	67*	14	39-95	...		
Arkansas	36	7	22-50	...		
Connecticut	49*	25	0-98	...		
Georgia	30*	9	14-47	...		
Illinois	54*	22	9-98	...		
Indiana	54*	14	26-82	...		
Iowa	52	10	33-71	...		
Kansas	38	7	25-51	...		
Kentucky	53	15	23-83	...		
Louisiana	75*	29	18-132	...		
Maine	63	17	30-96	39*	9	21-56
Maryland	71*	28	14-127	...		
Massachusetts	48*	17	15-82	...		
Michigan	53	11	33-74	...		
Minnesota	46	10	26-65	...		
Mississippi	69*	41	−11-149	28*	10	10-47
Missouri	36	8	21-51	68*	17	34-101
Nebraska	92	24	44-139	...		
Nevada	73*	35	5-141	...		
New Hampshire	40	10	21-59	143*	74	−4-289
New Mexico	86	37	13-158	...		
New York	47	11	26-68	111*	45	23-200
North Carolina	58*	15	27-88	...		
North Dakota	47	5	36-58	...		
Ohio	79	18	43-114	...		
Oklahoma	56	19	21-92	...		
Pennsylvania	47	7	33-60	116*	29	58-174
South Carolina	35	9	19-52	...		
South Dakota	67	13	42-92	...		
Tennessee	33*	7	19-47	23*	7	10-36
Texas	76	16	46-107	122*	37	49-195
Utah	53	8	38-69	...		
Vermont	28	4	19-35	21*	8	5-37
Virginia	104*	42	21-186	60*	62	−61-181
Washington	54	11	33-75	...		
West Virginia	52	12	30-76	62*	26	11-113
Wisconsin	46	6	34-58	76*	56	−33-186

... Sample size too small to report data reliably.
* Sample size based on a small sample size of 10-29.
Note: The sample sizes for California, Delaware, Florida, New Jersey, and Rhode Island were too small to report state resident values reliably.

Table 2. Elk Hunting Net Economic Values Per Day: 2001

	State Resident Values			Out-of-Stater's Values		
	Dollars per Day	Standard Error	95% Confidence Interval	Dollars per Day	Standard Error	95% Confidence Interval
Aggregate	84	15	55-113	120	32	57-182
Colorado	112	61	–9-232	110*	51	9-211
Idaho	60	17	26-94	...		
Montana	86	31	26-147	...		
Oregon	76	13	51-102	...		
Wyoming	61	13	36-86	...		

... Sample size too small to report data reliably.
* Sample size based on a small sample size of 10-29.

Table 3. Moose Hunting Net Economic Values Per Day: 2001

	State Resident Values			Out-of-Stater's Values		
	Dollars per Day	Standard Error	95% Confidence Interval	Dollars per Day	Standard Error	95% Confidence Interval
Alaska	118*	28	61-174	...		

... Sample size too small to report data reliably.
* Sample size based on a small sample size of 10-29.

Table 4. Bass Fishing Net Economic Values Per Day: 2001

	State Resident Values			Out-of-Stater's Values		
	Dollars per Day	Standard Error	95% Confidence Interval	Dollars per Day	Standard Error	95% Confidence Interval
Aggregate	48	3	41-54	72	10	52-92
Alabama	31	8	15-47	63*	49	–32-158
Arkansas	61	15	33-90	49*	22	7-92
Delaware	30*	9	13-48	...		
Florida	67	20	28-106	53*	22	11-96
Georgia	55	19	19-91	...		
Illinois	52	19	17-88	...		
Indiana	36	7	22-49	...		
Iowa	34	9	16-52	...		
Kansas	20	4	13-29	...		
Kentucky	61	22	17-105	216*	104	11-420
Louisiana	43	15	14-72	...		
Maryland	87	44	2-173	42*	22	–2-85
Massachusetts	36	11	14-58	...		
Mississippi	29	7	16-42	...		
Missouri	52	12	30-76	48*	7	35-61
Nebraska	37	7	23-51	...		
North Carolina	52*	25	3-101	31*	11	10-53
Oklahoma	33	8	18-48	...		
Rhode Island	24*	7	11-38	...		
South Carolina	58	16	26-89	...		
Tennessee	53	18	18-88	55*	15	25-85
Texas	56	22	12-99	97*	52	–6-200
Virginia	25	5	14-36	56*	38	–18-130
West Virginia	25	6	14-37	...		

... Sample size too small to report data reliably.
* Estimate based on a small sample size of 10-29.

Table 5. Trout Fishing Net Economic Values Per Day: 2001

	State Resident Values			Out-of-Stater's Values		
	Dollars per Day	Standard Error	95% Confidence Interval	Dollars per Day	Standard Error	95% Confidence Interval
Aggregate	51	3	45-57	91	13	65-116
Alaska	85	32	22-148	...		
Arizona	52	10	33-71	...		
California	58	9	40-76	52	16	21-83
Colorado	53	13	28-79	56	9	40-73
Connecticut	33	11	12-55	...		
Idaho	60	19	24-97	162	87	−7-332
Maine	53	14	25-81	88*	41	7-169
Montana	31	5	20-41	184	61	64-304
Nevada	43	11	22-64	...		
New Hampshire	35	6	22-47	95*	37	23-168
New Jersey	56*	28	1-111	...		
New Mexico	68	26	15-119	...		
New York	38*	14	10-66	123*	44	36-209
Oregon	40	13	15-65	62*	18	27-97
Pennsylvania	61	25	12-110	81*	38	6-155
Utah	44	9	27-61	69*	14	41-97
Vermont	29	8	13-45	...		
Washington	44	8	29-60	...		
Wyoming	38	7	25-52	63	17	31-96

... Sample size too small to report data reliably.
* Estimate based on a small sample size of 10-29.

Table 6. Walleye Fishing Net Economic Values Per Day: 2001

	State Resident Values			Out-of-Stater's Values		
	Dollars per Day	Standard Error	95% Confidence Interval	Dollars per Day	Standard Error	95% Confidence Interval
Aggregate	44	6	32-57	75	11	53-96
Michigan	26*	8	11-41	...		
Minnesota	48	11	27-69	70	11	48-92
North Dakota	37	12	13-61	26*	12	4-50
Ohio	45	9	26-63	...		
South Dakota	30	4	21-39	44*	16	13-75
Wisconsin	52	26	2-103	81*	26	31-131

... Sample size too small to report data reliably.
* Estimate based on a small sample size of 10-29.

Table 7. Wildlife Watching Net Economic Values Per Day: 2001

	State Resident Values			Out-of-Stater's Values		
	Dollars per Day	Standard Error	95% Confidence Interval	Dollars per Day	Standard Error	95% Confidence Interval
Aggregate	35	2	32-39	134	12	110-158
Alabama	31*	15	2-61	...		
Alaska	114	45	26-202	...		
Arizona	34	6	21-46	...		
Arkansas	20*	9	2-37	...		
California	39	8	24-54	64*	14	36-91
Colorado	33	7	20-46	290*	211	–122-703
Connecticut	18	4	11-27	...		
Delaware	10*	4	3-19	...		
Florida	41	19	4-77	192*	85	24-359
Georgia	51*	20	14-90	...		
Hawaii	29*	9	11-46	...		
Idaho	26	10	6-46	117*	84	–49-282
Illinois	11*	2	7-15	63*	26	12-114
Indiana	36	9	18-53	...		
Iowa	20*	6	8-32	...		
Kansas	35	16	4-66	...		
Kentucky	26*	13	–1-52	...		
Louisiana	38*	11	16-59	...		
Maine	35	16	4-67	139*	47	47-231
Maryland	66	18	30-101	116*	44	30-203
Massachusetts	21*	4	14-28	73*	33	8-137
Michigan	23*	7	8-37	...		
Minnesota	46*	33	–18-111	...		
Missouri	19	3	13-25	...		
Montana	18	4	11-25	...		
Nebraska	57	20	20-96	...		
Nevada	41*	16	9-73	...		
New Hampshire	27	7	14-40	151*	61	32-271
New Jersey	34	6	22-46	...		
New Mexico	42	8	27-57	...		
New York	52	20	11-92	75*	26	26-125
North Carolina	55*	28	–2-111	90*	41	9-171
North Dakota	33*	12	11-57	...		
Ohio	22	4	12-31	...		
Oklahoma	18*	3	13-24	...		
Oregon	34	7	22-47	120*	60	3-237
Pennsylvania	31	10	12-50	145*	55	37-252
Rhode Island	29*	16	–1-60	...		
South Carolina	29*	11	8-50	...		
South Dakota	22*	5	11-33	...		
Tennessee	19*	5	9-29	322*	143	42-602
Texas	34*	15	5-64	...		
Utah	27	6	16-39	96*	27	44-148
Vermont	38	21	–3-79	134*	85	–34-301
Virginia	55*	14	27-83	185*	61	64-305
Washington	50	8	33-66	78*	27	23-132
West Virginia	47*	35	–21-115	...		
Wisconsin	44	11	23-65	...		
Wyoming	31	10	13-50	54*	28	–1-109

... Sample size too small to report data reliably.
* Sample size based on a small sample size of 10-29.
Note: The sample size for Mississippi was too small to report the state resident value reliably.

**Summary Table. States with Significant Differences in
Net Economic Values Over Time**
(2001 dollars)

	1980 Dollars/day	1985 Dollars/day	2001 Dollars/day
Deer hunting			
Alabama	32	41	110
Bass fishing			
Arkansas		20	61
Florida		21	67
Indiana		18	36
Nebraska		17	37
South Carolina		21	52
Trout fishing			
Arizona	24		52
California	34		58
Maine	19		53
New Hampshire	15		35
Utah	24		44
Washington	24		44
Wildlife watching			
Delaware		41	10
Idaho		68	26
Illinois		31	11
Montana		31	18
Tennessee		56	19

Note: The 1980 Survey did not measure net economic values for bass fishing or wildlife watching and the 1985 Survey did not measure values for trout fishing.

State Comparisons in Net Economic Values Over Time

State-by-state comparisons of deer hunting, bass and trout fishing, and wildlife watching values for 1980, 1985, and 2001 show nearly all values to be similar. See the Summary Table at left for the few states that had significant differences (at the .05 level of significance) in values over time.

The similar estimates from the 1980's compared to 2001 show that these estimates are stable, making them reliable indicators of the value of wildlife-related recreation.

It should be noted that the 1980 and 1985 values were for state residents participating anywhere in the U.S., while the 2001 values were for state residents participating in their state of residence. Given that for any given year most participation occurs within the resident state, this difference in methodology is not critical.

Of all the designated deer hunting states, only Alabama had a 2001 value that was significantly higher than those of 1980 and 1985 (Table 8). None of the 2001 numbers were significantly lower (at the .05 significance) than the 1980 and 1985 values. There are no value comparisons with the 1991 and 1996 Surveys because there were no values at the state level from the 1996 Survey, and the 1991 Survey used the dichotomous method, which is a significantly different approach to valuing wildlife-related recreation. All dollar values in this report are in 2001 dollars.

Table 8. Deer Hunting 1980, 1985, and 2001 Values Per Day
(2001 Dollars)

	State Resident Values			Out-of-Stater's Values
	1980 Dollars/day	1985 Dollars/day	2001 Dollars/day	2001 Dollars/day
Alabama	32	41	110*	57*+
Arizona	52	64	67*	...
Arkansas	37	50	36	...
California	54	69	...	...
Connecticut	39	51	49*	...
Delaware	43	41	...	...
Florida	34	89	...	...
Georgia	37	45	30*	...
Illinois	47	54	54*	...
Indiana	32	45	54*	...
Iowa	37	61	52	...
Kansas	34	40	38	...
Kentucky	45	53	53	...
Louisiana	41	45	75*	...
Maine	30	40	63	39*
Maryland	47	64	71*	...
Massachusetts	39	69	48*	...
Michigan	32	56	53	...
Minnesota	43	51	46	...
Mississippi	32	36	69*+	28*
Missouri	39	43	36	68*
Nebraska	47	53	92	...
Nevada	60	96	73*	...
New Hampshire	28	35	40	143*
New Jersey	45	61	...	...
New Mexico	60	81	86	...
New York	32	40	47	111*
North Carolina	39	40	58*	...
North Dakota	49	46	47	...
Ohio	43	46	79	...
Oklahoma	43	56	56	...
Pennsylvania	45	53	47	116*
Rhode Island	41*	64*	...	...
South Carolina	32	43	35	...
South Dakota	49	43	67	...
Tennessee	30	48	33*	23*
Texas	56	64	76	122*
Utah	43	68	53	...
Vermont	30	35	28	21*
Virginia	34	45	104*	60*+
Washington	37	46	54	...
West Virginia	43	51	52	62*
Wisconsin	34	53	46	76*+

... Sample size too small to report data reliably.
* Sample size based on a small sample size of 10-29.
+ 95% confidence interval includes zero.

Table 9. Bass Fishing 1985 and 2001 Values Per Day
(2001 dollars)

	State Resident Values		Out-of-Stater's Values
	1985 Dollars/day	2001 Dollars/day	2001 Dollars/day
Alabama	21	31	63*+
Arkansas	20	61	49*
Delaware	21	30*	...
Florida	21	67	53*
Georgia	23	55	...
Illinois	36	52	...
Indiana	18	36	...
Iowa	17	34	...
Kansas	17*	20	...
Kentucky	21	61	216*
Louisiana	33	43	...
Maryland	23	87	42*
Massachusetts	15	36	...
Mississippi	15	29	...
Missouri	31	52	48*
Nebraska	17	37	...
North Carolina	21	52*	31*
Oklahoma	18	33	...
Rhode Island	21	24*	...
South Carolina	15	58	...
Tennessee	18	53	55*
Texas	31	56	97*
Virginia	20	25	56*+
West Virginia	21	25	...

... Sample size too small to report data reliably.
* Estimate based on a small sample size of 10-29.
+ 95% confidence interval includes zero.

For the designated bass fishing states, 5 of 24 states had 2001 values that were significantly higher than 1985 values (Table 9). These states were Arkansas, Florida, Indiana, Nebraska, and South Carolina. There were no decreases in values for bass fishing by state.

Six of 19 states with trout fishing values for 1980 and 2001 had 2001 values that were significantly higher than 1980 values (Table 10). These states were Arizona, California, Maine, New Hampshire, Utah, and Washington. There were no decreases from 1980 to 2001 in trout fishing values by state.

Table 10. Trout Fishing 1980 and 2001 Values Per Day
(2001 dollars)

	State Resident Values		Out-of-Stater's Values
	1980 Dollars/day	2001 Dollars/day	2001 Dollars/day
Alaska	60*	85	...
Arizona	24	52	...
California	34	58	52
Colorado	28	53	56
Connecticut	17	33	...
Idaho	22	60	162
Maine	19	53	88*
Montana	26	31	184
Nevada	24	43	...
New Hampshire	15	35	95*
New Jersey	22	56*	...
New Mexico	30	68	...
New York	19	38*	123*
Oregon	26	40	62*
Pennsylvania	17	61	81*
Utah	24	44	69*
Vermont	15	29	...
Washington	24	44	...
Wyoming	32	38	63

... Sample size too small to report data reliably.
* Estimate based on a small sample size of 10-29.

Table 11. Wildlife Watching 1985 and 2001 Values Per Day
(2001 Dollars)

	State Resident Values		Out-of-Stater's Values
	1985 Dollars/day	*2001* Dollars/day	*2001* Dollars/day
Alabama	21	31*	...
Alaska	40	114	...
Arizona	50	34	...
Arkansas	20	20*	...
California	53	39	64*
Colorado	43	33	290*
Connecticut	31	18	...
Delaware	41	10*	...
Florida	26	41	192*
Georgia	43	51*	...
Hawaii	45	29*	...
Idaho	68	26	117*
Illinois	31	11*	63*
Indiana	46	36	...
Iowa	21	20*	...
Kansas	23	35	...
Kentucky	25	26*	...
Louisiana	17	38*	...
Maine	17	35	139*
Maryland	40	66	116*
Massachusetts	35	21	73*
Michigan	33	23*	...
Minnesota	33	46*+	...
Mississippi	20	...	...
Missouri	23	19	...
Montana	31	18	...
Nebraska	18	57	...
Nevada	41	41*	...
New Hampshire	30	27	151*
New Jersey	46	34	...
New Mexico	48	42	...
New York	26	52	75*
North Carolina	23	55*	90*
North Dakota	36	33*	...
Ohio	21	22	...
Oklahoma	18	18*	...
Oregon	25	34	120*
Pennsylvania	40	31	145*
Rhode Island	35	29*	...
South Carolina	56	29*	...
South Dakota	21	22*	...
Tennessee	56	19*	322*
Texas	40	34*	...
Utah	35	27	96*
Vermont	30	38+	134*
Virginia	35	55*	185*
Washington	33	50	78*
West Virginia	28	47*+	...
Wisconsin	25*	44	...
Wyoming	38	31	54*

... Sample size too small to report data reliably.
* Sample size based on a small sample size of 10-29.
+ 95% confidence interval includes zero.

Five of 49 states with wildlife-watching values for 1985 and 2001 had 2001 values that were significantly lower than 1985 values (Table 11). These states were Delaware, Idaho, Illinois, Montana, and Tennessee. In no state were there statistically significantly higher estimates in 2001 compared to 1985.

V. Using the Value Estimates

When and how can these values be used? These numbers are appropriate for any project evaluation that seeks to quantify benefits and costs. They can be used to evaluate management actions that increase or decrease participation. Two types of willingness-to-pay values are available, net economic values per day per participant and net economic values per year of participation. Each of these values has a slightly different use and interpretation in conducting benefit and cost calculations of wildlife management and policy decisions.

Mean net economic values per year per participant can be thought of as "all or nothing values." Take trout fishing in Montana as an example, with a mean value of $282 (Table B-5 in Appendix B). The $282 represents the mean value to a resident trout angler in Montana given the current resource condition and trout fishing regulations. This is like the estimate of net economic value portrayed in Figure 1. If a wildlife refuge in Montana changes its policies and allows 100 more trout anglers to visit per year, the total value to society due to this policy change would be $28,200 ($282 × 100) per year (assuming all visitors are state residents). This value, however, assumes that these 100 anglers could and would fish for trout only at this refuge and that they would take a certain number of trips to this refuge. Thus, while mean net economic values per year per participant are interesting in terms of characterizing the current value of the resource and in calculating losses for a catastrophic change in the resource, they are not applicable for most management and public policy decisions faced by resource managers.

Management and policy actions generally increase or decrease participation. Let us continue with the Montana example. Assume an environmental pollution accident results in the closure of a lake to fishing for a whole season. If a fishery manager knows the number of days of state resident fishing that occur on the lake over the whole season, 1,200 for example, it is possible to develop a rough estimate of the fishery losses from the accident. This estimate is accomplished by multiplying the net economic value per day ($31 from Table 5) by the days of participation, resulting in $37,200 ($31 × 1,200). If the refuge had data on the number of in-state and out-of-state visitors then the numbers could be adjusted to reflect their appropriate value.

Two caveats exist to the examples above: (1) if recreationists can shift their activity to another location then the values are an overestimate; and (2) if a loss of wildlife habitat causes an overall degradation in the number of game, fish, or wildlife and in the quality of wildlife-related recreation then the values are an underestimate.

The key issues that must be understood are:

- Each of the different value estimates has slightly different interpretations and uses;

- If an action changes participation, it is necessary to consider the extent to which participants substitute another site to fish, hunt, or wildlife watch. Failure to consider substitution will result in overestimation of resource losses; and

- Using per participant value estimates to compute losses or benefits requires additional information, particularly on resource conditions and participation rates.

Thus, the value estimates reported here must be used with caution in order to avoid misuse, which would result in incorrect estimates of aggregate costs or aggregate benefits.

USFWS

VI. Concluding Comments

Contingent valuation questions in the 2001 National Survey of Fishing, Hunting, and Wildlife-Associated Recreation provide a nationwide data base for estimating net economic recreation values for selected wildlife-related recreation activities on a state-by-state basis. The data and the values they produce are important because they measure recreationists' net willingness to pay for such activities, the conceptually correct measure of net economic value for a wide range of analyses and project evaluations. Because they are available for individual states, the values allow for differences in recreation values in various parts of the country. For many kinds of analysis, using values that reflect wildlife-related recreation in the state in question rather than some other state or a national average gives the analysis a better and more convincing empirical base.

In this age of cost-benefit analysis these estimates can be used to justify the value of wildlife-related recreation. Be it deer hunting, trout fishing, or wildlife watching, the numbers prove that Americans benefit greatly from wildlife.

Fred Deines, USFWS

Appendix A. Contingent Valuation Questions from the 2001 National Survey of Fishing, Hunting, and Wildlife-Associated Recreation

Hunting Economic Evaluation[1]
In the next few questions, I will ask you about ALL your trips taken during the ENTIRE calendar year of 2001 to PRIMARILY hunt for [fill GAME] in [fill I_RESIDENT].

Sometimes you may take [fill TEMP1] [fill GAME] hunting trip where you are away from home one night or several nights. Other times, you may take [fill TEMP1] [fill GAME] hunting trip where you leave from and return to your home in one day. In total, how many trips did you take to hunt PRIMARILY for [fill GAME] during 2001 in [fill I_RESIDENT]?

Think about what it costs you for a TYPICAL [fill GAME] hunting trip. Include your expenses for things such as gasoline and other transportation costs, food, and lodging. If you went hunting with family or friends, include ONLY YOUR SHARE of the cost.

Keeping all those expenses in mind, how much did a TYPICAL hunting trip cost you during 2001 when you hunted PRIMARILY for [fill GAME] in [fill I_RESIDENT]?

What is the most your [fill GAME] hunting in [fill I_RESIDENT] could have cost you per trip last year before you would NOT have gone [fill GAME] hunting at all in 2001, not even one trip, because it would have been too expensive?

Keep in mind that the cost per trip of other kinds of hunting, fishing and recreational activities would not have changed.

So, in other words, $[fill HUNTBID] would have been too much to pay for one [fill GAME] hunting trip last year in [fill I_RESIDENT]?

    (1) Yes
    (2) No

[If No,]
How much would have been too much to pay for one [fill GAME] hunting trip last year in [fill I_RESIDENT]?

Wildlife-Watching Economic Evaluation
In the next few questions, I will ask you about ALL your trips taken for the PRIMARY PURPOSE of observing, photographing, or feeding wildlife during the ENTIRE calendar year of 2001 in [fill I_RESIDENT].

In your [fill TEMP1] you reported taking [fill ECONADD] [trip/trips] for the PRIMARY PURPOSE of observing, photographing, or feeding wildlife in [fill I_RESIDENT]. Is that correct?

    (1) Yes
    (2) No

[If No,]
How many trips did you take for the PRIMARY PURPOSE of observing, feeding or photographing wildlife in [fill I_RESIDENT] during 2001?

In your [fill TEMP1], you reported that you spent on average $[fill NCUTOT] per trip during 2001 where your PRIMARY PURPOSE was to observe, photograph or feed wildlife in [fill I_RESIDENT]. Would you say that cost is about right?

    (1) Yes
    (2) No

[If No,]
How much would you say was the average cost of your [fill TEMP1] [trip/trips] during 2001 where your PRIMARY PURPOSE was to observe, photograph, or feed wildlife in [fill I_RESIDENT]? If you went with family or friends, include ONLY YOUR SHARE of the cost.

What is the most your trip(s) to observe, photograph, or feed wildlife in [fill I_RESIDENT] could have cost you per trip last year before you would NOT have gone at all in 2001, not even one trip, because it would have been too expensive?

Keep in mind that the cost per trip of other kinds of recreation would not have changed.

So, in other words, $[fill ECONNCU] would have been too much to pay to take even one trip to observe, photograph, or feed wildlife in 2001 in [fill I_RESIDENT]?

    (1) Yes
    (2) No

[If No,]
How much would have been too much to pay to take even 1 trip to feed, photograph, or observe wildlife in 2001 in [fill I_RESIDENT]?

---

[1] The fishing economic evaluation questions were the same as the hunting questions.

Note: All bracketed fill commands were provided by the computer for each interview.

Appendix B. Annual Net Economic Values

Table B-1. Deer Hunting Net Economic Value Per Year: 2001

	State Resident Values			Out-of-Stater's Values		
	Dollars per Year	Standard Error	95% Confidence Interval	Dollars per Year	Standard Error	95% Confidence Interval
Aggregate	377	15	347-406	331	29	274-387
Alabama	858*	292	287-1,429	499*	297	-83-1,081
Arizona	349*	111	131-567	...		
Arkansas	331	81	172-489	...		
Connecticut	529*	225	87-971	...		
Georgia	456*	107	246-666	...		
Illinois	456*	186	91-820	...		
Indiana	588*	192	211-965	...		
Iowa	210	60	94-327	...		
Kansas	307	111	90-524	...		
Kentucky	271	58	157-385	...		
Louisiana	449*	110	233-664	...		
Maine	420	81	262-579	289*	108	77-500
Maryland	392*	169	61-723	...		
Massachusetts	307*	67	176-438	...		
Michigan	433	95	246-619	...		
Minnesota	238	47	146-330	...		
Mississippi	400*	160	86-714	211*	49	116-306
Missouri	198	46	108-288	209*	53	105-314
Nebraska	475	99	281-669	...		
Nevada	321*	152	21-620	...		
New Hampshire	402	173	65-740	586*	265	65-1,106
New Mexico	389	183	29-749	...		
New York	485	104	282-688	282*	82	120-444
North Carolina	657*	170	323-991	...		
North Dakota	284	53	178-389	...		
Ohio	350	62	229-471	...		
Oklahoma	668	156	362-974	...		
Pennsylvania	247	50	151-344	343*	87	171-514
South Carolina	408	101	209-606	...		
South Dakota	309	60	192-426	...		
Tennessee	313*	124	68-557	140*	51	40-240
Texas	418	82	256-580	550*	258	46-1,055
Utah	220	29	162-277	...		
Vermont	258	53	155-362	92*	29	35-149
Virginia	675*	247	191-1,160	98*	60	-19-215
Washington	277	43	194-360	...		
West Virginia	295	55	186-403	501*	197	115-886
Wisconsin	335	45	245-424	379*	91	201-557

... Sample size too small to report data reliably.
* Estimate based on a small sample size of 10-29.
Note: The sample sizes for California, Delaware, Florida, New Jersey, and Rhode Island were too small to report state resident values reliably.

Table B-2. Elk Hunting Net Economic Value Per Year: 2001

| | State Resident Values | | | | Out-of-Stater's Values | | |
	Dollars per Year	Standard Error	95% Confidence Interval		Dollars per Year	Standard Error	95% Confidence Interval
Aggregate	380	43	296-464		556	148	266-845
Colorado	252	64	127-377		604*	256	103-1,106
Idaho	347	100	150-544		...		
Montana	316	67	183-448		...		
Oregon	552	120	317-786		...		
Wyoming	414	138	144-684		...		

... Sample size too small to report data reliably.
* Estimate based on a small sample size of 10-29.

Table B-3. Moose Hunting Net Economic Value Per Year: 2001

| | State Resident Values | | | | Out-of-Stater's Values | | |
	Dollars per Year	Standard Error	95% Confidence Interval		Dollars per Year	Standard Error	95% Confidence Interval
Alaska	579*	126	331-826		...		

... Sample size too small to report data reliably.
* Estimate based on a small sample size of 10-29.

Table B-4. Bass Fishing Net Economic Values Per Year: 2001

| | State Resident Values | | | | Out-of-Stater's Values | | |
	Dollars per Year	Standard Error	95% Confidence Interval		Dollars per Year	Standard Error	95% Confidence Interval
Aggregate	370	21	329-410		257	29	201-313
Alabama	358	79	203-513		135*	62	14-257
Arkansas	638	202	241-1,034		400*	169	69-732
Delaware	287*	212	-129-703		...		
Florida	569	127	322-817		286*	93	104-468
Georgia	266	45	177-354		...		
Illinois	397	86	227-566		...		
Indiana	285	60	169-402		...		
Iowa	155	34	88-222		...		
Kansas	163	38	87-238		...		
Kentucky	432	125	187-677		413*	141	136-690
Louisiana	295	63	173-418		...		
Maryland	433	113	210-654		187*	80	30-343
Massachusetts	284	64	159-409		...		
Mississippi	248	57	137-360		...		
Missouri	449	94	264-634		184*	47	92-276
Nebraska	251	45	162-340		...		
North Carolina	279*	62	158-400		123*	63	-2-247
Oklahoma	347	79	193-501		...		
Rhode Island	271*	129	18-524		...		
South Carolina	488	123	246-729		...		
Tennessee	409	112	190-629		601*	244	122-1,079
Texas	397	123	155-638		286*	104	82-490
Virginia	214	46	123-305		174*	108	-37-386
West Virginia	205	51	105-305		...		

... Sample size too small to report data reliably.
* Estimate based on a small sample size of 10-29.

Table B-5. Trout Fishing Net Economic Values Per Year: 2001

	State Resident Values			Out-of-Stater's Values		
	Dollars per Year	Standard Error	95% Confidence Interval	Dollars per Year	Standard Error	95% Confidence Interval
Aggregate	300	14	272-328	325	33	259-390
Alaska	411	104	208-615	...		
Arizona	277	45	187-366	...		
California	287	51	186-387	260	77	109-411
Colorado	331	60	213-449	273	43	188-356
Connecticut	199	37	127-271	...		
Idaho	267	60	148-385	316	127	69-564
Maine	337	80	180-494	350*	90	173-527
Montana	282	53	177-386	677	203	279-1,074
Nevada	364	109	151-578	...		
New Hampshire	347	59	230-463	527*	226	83-970
New Jersey	401*	176	56-746	...		
New Mexico	301	88	128-474	...		
New York	286*	87	115-456	513*	271	−18-1,044
Oregon	216	39	140-293	134*	55	26-242
Pennsylvania	400	107	189-610	293*	111	76-511
Utah	232	27	179-284	225*	77	74-376
Vermont	250	66	122-379	...		
Washington	301	56	191-410	...		
Wyoming	351	50	255-448	210	55	103-318

... Sample size too small to report data reliably.
* Estimate based on a small sample size of 10-29.

Table B-6. Walleye Fishing Net Economic Values Per Year: 2001

	State Resident Values			Out-of-Stater's Values		
	Dollars per Year	Standard Error	95% Confidence Interval	Dollars per Year	Standard Error	95% Confidence Interval
Aggregate	335	27	282-389	350	50	253-447
Michigan	200*	76	51-349	...		
Minnesota	427	66	299-556	350	67	221-481
North Dakota	237	33	172-302	155*	135	−110-420
Ohio	202	41	121-283	...		
South Dakota	324	63	200-448	235*	97	45-424
Wisconsin	375	92	195-556	409*	146	123-695

... Sample size too small to report data reliably.
* Estimate based on a small sample size of 10-29.

Table B-7. Wildlife Watching Net Economic Values Per Year: 2001

	State Resident Values			Out-of-Stater's Values		
	Dollars per Year	*Standard Error*	*95% Confidence Interval*	*Dollars per Year*	*Standard Error*	*95% Confidence Interval*
Aggregate	257	12	233-282	488	37	415-561
Alabama	242*	94	59-426	...		
Alaska	722	192	345-1,099	...		
Arizona	272	59	156-388	...		
Arkansas	192*	111	−26-409	...		
California	230	51	130-331	176*	59	62-292
Colorado	257	75	109-405	737*	209	327-1,147
Connecticut	252	112	34-471	...		
Delaware	73*	33	9-137	...		
Florida	313	99	119-507	808*	260	297-1,318
Georgia	389*	203	−10-787	...		
Hawaii	243*+	135	−21-507	...		
Idaho	112	47	21-204	344*	245	−136-824
Illinois	93*	20	52-133	347*	140	74-621
Indiana	428	177	82-775	...		
Iowa	194	103	−6-395	...		
Kansas	289	152	−10-586	...		
Kentucky	214*	63	90-337	...		
Louisiana	268*	108	56-479	...		
Maine	282	88	111-454	610*	213	191-1,028
Maryland	362	94	178-546	722*	263	206-1,238
Massachusetts	208	63	85-332	227*	234	−233-686
Michigan	289*	81	130-447	...		
Minnesota	323*	147	33-612	...		
Missouri	131	57	20-243	...		
Montana	178	43	95-261	...		
Nebraska	198	55	89-306	...		
Nevada	381*+	217	−45-807	...		
New Hampshire	178	51	78-278	470*	195	87-853
New Jersey	198	38	124-273	...		
New Mexico	328	85	161-494	...		
New York	305	73	164-447	173*	67	42-305
North Carolina	493*+	302	−99-1,085	529*	374	−205-1,262
North Dakota	190*	58	77-303	...		
Ohio	170	59	54-286	...		
Oklahoma	141*	60	23-259	...		
Oregon	267	52	164-370	630*	291	60-1,200
Pennsylvania	299	84	134-464	458*	263	−56-973
Rhode Island	237*+	214	−182-656	...		
South Carolina	239*	67	110-370	...		
South Dakota	181*	89	7-355	...		
Tennessee	130*	39	55-206	629*	232	173-1,084
Texas	208*	68	74-342	...		
Utah	221	49	126-316	230*	91	51-409
Vermont	192	68	59-325	561*	257	57-1,065
Virginia	316*	81	159-474	510*	122	270-750
Washington	323	72	183-463	339*	82	177-501
West Virginia	278*	113	57-499	...		
Wisconsin	299	71	160-438	...		
Wyoming	184	58	71-297	259*	125	15-504

... Sample size too small to report data reliably.
* Sample size based on a small sample size of 10-29.
Note: The sample size for Mississippi was too small to report state resident values reliably.

Appendix C. Sample Sizes

Table C-1. Sample Sizes for Deer Hunting

	State Residents	Out-of-Stater's
Alabama	29	11
Arizona	22	1
Arkansas	44	4
California	3	1
Connecticut	11	2
Delaware	8	0
Florida	8	2
Georgia	25	9
Illinois	12	6
Indiana	28	6
Iowa	44	3
Kansas	32	4
Kentucky	41	3
Louisiana	21	2
Maine	56	16
Maryland	21	4
Massachusetts	20	1
Michigan	51	6
Minnesota	55	8
Mississippi	19	13
Missouri	49	11
Nebraska	60	2
Nevada	14	2
New Hampshire	37	10
New Jersey	7	1
New Mexico	32	1
New York	39	16
North Carolina	21	4
North Dakota	106	2
Ohio	43	7
Oklahoma	39	2
Pennsylvania	67	29
Rhode Island	4	0
South Carolina	35	4
South Dakota	51	5
Tennessee	19	11
Texas	41	11
Utah	88	2
Vermont	48	10
Virginia	27	10
Washington	56	1
West Virginia	60	15
Wisconsin	90	11

Table C-2. Sample Sizes for Elk Hunting

	State Residents	Out-of-Stater's
Colorado	34	18
Idaho	33	3
Montana	83	6
Oregon	53	2
Wyoming	37	4

Table C-3. Sample Sizes for Moose Hunting

	State Residents	Out-of-Stater's
Alaska	19	2

Table C-4. Sample Sizes for Bass Fishing

	State Residents	Out-of-Stater's
Alabama	76	15
Arkansas	46	12
Delaware	18	2
Florida	32	19
Georgia	40	6
Illinois	34	3
Indiana	52	8
Iowa	45	5
Kansas	61	6
Kentucky	56	13
Louisiana	39	8
Maryland	31	10
Massachusetts	37	5
Mississippi	53	6
Missouri	55	29
Nebraska	54	5
North Carolina	29	12
Oklahoma	60	6
Rhode Island	18	0
South Carolina	63	4
Tennessee	40	16
Texas	46	12
Virginia	41	10
West Virginia	30	4

Table C-5. Sample Sizes for Trout Fishing

	State Residents	Out-of-Stater's
Alaska	73	3
Arizona	61	8
California	75	32
Colorado	130	61
Connecticut	41	1
Idaho	89	51
Maine	50	11
Montana	98	36
Nevada	44	3
New Hampshire	59	17
New Jersey	18	0
New Mexico	74	4
New York	20	19
Oregon	105	21
Pennsylvania	47	28
Utah	226	29
Vermont	37	7
Washington	132	5
Wyoming	98	48

Table C-6. Sample Sizes for Walleye Fishing

	State Residents	Out-of-Stater's
Michigan	23	8
Minnesota	73	58
North Dakota	133	11
Ohio	41	6
South Dakota	78	18
Wisconsin	69	18

Table C-7. Sample Sizes for Wildlife Watching

	State Residents	Out-of-Stater's
Alabama	29	3
Alaska	43	3
Arizona	44	9
Arkansas	18	2
California	54	17
Colorado	49	14
Connecticut	37	4
Delaware	13	2
Florida	33	24
Georgia	11	3
Hawaii	14	4
Idaho	32	14
Illinois	24	10
Indiana	33	3
Iowa	28	1
Kansas	34	1
Kentucky	28	5
Louisiana	16	4
Maine	31	16
Maryland	41	14
Massachusetts	41	13
Michigan	23	7
Minnesota	15	4
Mississippi	4	1
Missouri	31	3
Montana	41	8
Nebraska	32	6
Nevada	22	3
New Hampshire	41	13
New Jersey	49	5
New Mexico	45	3
New York	35	19
North Carolina	19	10
North Dakota	20	1
Ohio	39	4
Oklahoma	25	3
Oregon	65	18
Pennsylvania	31	16
Rhode Island	21	2
South Carolina	24	0
South Dakota	23	7
Tennessee	23	10
Texas	14	5
Utah	62	14
Vermont	31	12
Virginia	25	16
Washington	91	21
West Virginia	17	1
Wisconsin	43	8
Wyoming	34	14